BREAKI *from the* TRENCHES OF THE MIND

GIVING BIRTH TO
A LIFE WITHOUT LIMITS

ReLease The Power
Within you.

Herman Hall

March 8, 2010

HERMAN HALL

Cover & Interior Design by Tarsha L. Campbell

DOMINIONHOUSE
Publishing & Design
P.O. Box 681938 | Orlando, Florida 32868 | 407.880.5790
www.mydominionhouse.com

The Lord gave the word: great was the company of those
that published it. (Psalms 68:11)

ACKNOWLEDGEMENT

You cannot take on a project of this magnitude without the support and commitment of those around you. Being a new writer I had to gain their trust and confidence in my ability to succeed. Without complaining, my supporters worked alongside me and made personal sacrifices to assist me in fulfilling my vision.

I'm thrilled to be working with my new publishing family at Dominionhouse and I'm grateful for their assistance in making this project exceed my expectation.

First and foremost, I want to thank my mom for her love and guidance and for all the sacrifices she had to make as a single parent. Even though physically she's no longer with me, her spirit of perseverance and principles will always be there to remind me that the trials of my faith are only there to make me stronger. Thanks mom; I love you.

Thanks to Stephanie Oliphant for your patience and input during the initial phase of getting this project off the ground. Thank you for your assistance, suggestions, and structure in helping me establish a foundation to work from. Thank you Evelyn Walker for keeping faith in me and for those last minute rush reviews and your valuable input. Thanks to Loretta Mercer-Fuller for your willingness to fit me into your busy schedule for last minute proofing.

Thanks to a host of encouragers: Shirley Wilson (sister), Ollie Wilson (brother-in-law), Elizabeth Thompson (sister), Pamela Murray, Karen Maxwell, and Frances Maxwell. You guys gave support and cheered me on during some of my most challenging times.

I would be remiss not to thank some incredible teachers: Pastor Mike Freeman, Pastor Dewayne Freeman, Pastor Delman Coates and Pastor Victor O. Kirk. Many times your wisdom was my strength.

Last, but not least, I have to acknowledge my end of book anchors; when I so desperately needed a quiet place to dot the last "I" and cross the last "T". James Hall (brother), with all your wisdom, and Mattie Hall (sister-in-law), with your love and support, you guys did something that only family can do. Thank you. Deborah Mercer-Wesley, you stepped in and single-handedly helped bring it all to a close. You were faithful when I was being faithless. You coordinated, made connections, worked on design and provided invaluable input and support.

TABLE OF CONTENTS

Acknowledgement

Introduction

• • • • • •

This book is saturated with self-empowering proverbs. It speaks to the trenches that are in our life's path and the stronghold they have over us. It alerts us to the danger of a distorted, fragmented mind and the destructive impact it can have on one's vision.

INTRODUCTION

This book is saturated with self-empowering proverbs. It speaks to the trenches that are in our life's path and the stronghold they have over us. It alerts us to the danger of a distorted, fragmented mind and the destructive impact it can have on one's vision. It starts you on a life journey of walking in love accompanied by good health, wealth and wisdom. It explains why you have God's favor in your life but, more importantly, it shows you how to tap into His continuous grace. It explains how God's original plan will always be His final intention and must be our only destination. It gives a complete account of what went wrong in the wilderness, and explores why an eleven-day trip took 40 years.

The material of this book covers subjects such as 'seedtime and harvest', by introducing new dimensions and bringing new meaning to the subject 'sowing seed'. It tells how the sower receives more than the one he's sowing to. It explains how undervaluing one's self causes false perceptions which interferes with God's plan for your life. However, it also emphasizes that with God's divine providential power and purpose for your life, success can be achieved for His will to be done. It explains how to operate at the highest physical form and reveals the culprit behind a dismantled relationship. You will view challenges in a whole new light. You will understand the true meaning behind struggles and challenges. You will see the importance of aligning your thoughts with God. And by doing so, God's creation in you continues. No longer will it be a mystery about the difference between believers and non-believers.

You will see how all your needs are met. And you will understand how you call that which is not into existence. You will get to hear a life-changing personal testimony of how a heart disease or disorder was not acknowledged and the miraculous way God's healing power was revealed.

This book is informative in many ways and on multiple levels. The feedback I received from proofreaders has already created enough inspiration to write the next volume. Your faith will be strengthened. Your spiritual awareness will increase. Your love will grow stronger for God, yourself and others. You will be blessed and thereby become a blessing to others through the sharing of the life altering self-awareness the reading of this book will truly bring.

The Trenches of The Mind is a place of unpleasant circumstances or challenges, where we find ourselves seemingly without the control to leave. A place the enemy is determined to keep and control us by the consequences that surround us. Get ready to emerge from this place, giving birth to a new life....a life without limits.

Mental Growth

• • • • • •

*Mental soundness is the umbrella
for emotional intelligence and
physical strength. Mental growth
is the catalyst and prerequisite for
bringing preconceived
ideas to reality.*

--Herman Hall

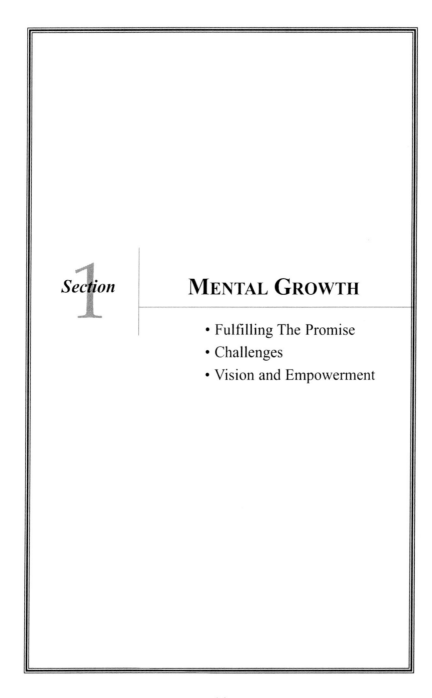

Section 1

MENTAL GROWTH

- Fulfilling The Promise
- Challenges
- Vision and Empowerment

Fulfilling The Promise

• • • • • •

God made a covenant with Abraham concerning his descendants. We are part of the descendants of Abraham and our purpose is not without His promises.

--Herman Hall

Chapter 1 | FULFILLING THE PROMISE

Breaking free and coming out of the Trenches ... transforming our thoughts into new things beyond those control mechanisms that are keeping us there.

Where do ideas begin and how do they end? Are they the dreams that were placed in us giving birth in their time and season? We are about to explore a little past, present and future. I start by asking the question "Is there a difference between resurrecting and creating"? When we read about the life of Abraham, we learn that he was fortunate enough to hear what God's plans were concerning his past, present and future. God said to Abraham that the land you are walking on (present), I created it for you (past), to give to your descendants, the children of Israel, after they are released from slavery (future). On that day, He said to Abraham:

> "Lift up now thine eyes, and look from the place
> where thou art northward, and southward, and
> eastward, and westward: For all the land which thou
> seest, to thee will I give it, and to thy seed forever.
> (Genesis 13:14-15 KJV)."

Most of us are well familiar with the story of Moses, how he was the one to fulfill the promise that was made to Abraham by leading the children of Israel from Egypt after being in slavery for 400 years, and 40 more years in the wilderness. Abraham was privileged to know what God was planning to do for the Israelites hundreds of years before it came to pass. The scripture reads like this:

> "And he said unto Abram, Know of a surety that thy
> seed shall be a stranger in a land that is not theirs,
> and shall serve them; and they shall afflict them four
> hundred years; And also that nation, whom they
> shall serve, will I judge: and afterward shall they
> come out with great substance. In the same day the
> Lord made a covenant with Abram, saying, Unto thy
> seed have I given this land, from the river of Egypt
> unto the great river, the river Euphrates. (Genesis
> 15: 13-14; 18, KJV)."

If you believe that God knew hundreds of years earlier that the children of Israel would occupy the land Abraham stood on, then surely you believe He knows our beginning and ending. Mediocrity and scarcity were not invited to this forum, because the next few pages are full of food for thought and provide plenty of growth opportunity for the mind, body and spirit.

14

"I am come that they might have life, and that they might have it more abundantly." (John 10:10, KJV).

From the pews of the church to the corporate boardroom, the power of positive thinking, law of attraction and unleashing the power of creation has captured the world's attention. More and more of us are learning that time is unfolding and/or resurrecting God's foretold plan for us. I use the word resurrecting because of a question, "is it created or is it planned". The Israelites did not have to create their way out of Egypt. Hundreds of years earlier their destiny had already been foretold. Everything from Moses going into Egypt to coming out of the wilderness was part of a plan. The only thing they had to do was let the promise that was made to Abraham, to bring them to the Promised Land, fulfill itself. We all are heirs to the promises that were made to Abraham. What good is being an heir or having an inheritance if you're not going to claim it? It was like the Israelites in the wilderness. They left Egypt as heirs to the promise land but never took ownership. Out of a million people that left Egypt, only two of the original ones, Joshua and Caleb, actually made it to the promise land. Why just two? Joshua and Caleb never stopped looking and never stopped believing in their reward during their trials. How often have we let an obstructed view cause us to terminate a predestined plan? There are good reasons for having obstructed views and detours in life. They build our confidence by teaching us to look for other ways to get things done.

To take it a step further, we are experiencing physically what's already part of a spiritual plan, the same as was with the life of Joseph. Everything he experienced was part of a process to put him in position to become second in command to Pharaoh. In many cases, a setback turns out to be a setup for better things. The hardest thing about a challenge is to understand its purpose. Did God (the Spirit) not tell Abraham about His plans (concerning the children of Israel) hundreds of years before time? Does that leave any doubt that there is already a spiritual plan in place for you and I? We can't become pilots, engineers, fishermen or anything else unless it is part of God's original plan. You will see in other parts of the book that God's original plan will always be His final intention. Your natural gifts and talents shouldn't come with difficult struggles. They are the seeds that were put in place that give birth to life's opportunities. We have heard, witnessed or known someone who has taken numerous singing lessons to find they still are not able to master the art of singing. Then there are others who start singing soon after they are able to talk. Some gifts are identified at an early age without any form of training. Whether they are identified early or later, natural gifts come without difficult struggles. We all have struggled in areas that we felt we shouldn't have. Or maybe you felt your struggle was lasting too long. Maybe what you were experiencing wasn't a struggle at all. Maybe it was just a challenge. Is there a difference between struggles and challenges? Struggles make no contribution to life, whereas challenges do.

In the beginning, I mentioned taking the word scarcity out of our thought process. The reason for doing that is because scarcity means a lack of or shortage of. Mediocrity and scarcity are two of the most dangerous, yet influential, words to the human mind. They are part of the reason why we struggle. Their messages range from "there's not enough", to "not deserving". And that message runs constantly in silence mode in your mind. Each of us provides a unique contribution to God's plan. Your unique blueprint was designed just for you. Your existence is evidence that God needed you in His master plan. That's how important your existence is. Everything has its place and time to reveal itself. Consider this as one of those times. Don't spend a lot of time trying to understand unexpected circumstances. View them from a different vantage point. Their whole purpose is to elevate you above your current condition. Keep in mind we are part of an ongoing creation. God is constantly doing a new thing through us, which for some is a cause for territory control. I understand that the thought of change, for some, is a feeling of being left behind. We are not here by chance or hope; we're here by purpose and promise. We are just as much a part of God's plan as was Abraham, Isaac and Jacob. This is your opportunity to stop accepting anything and start resurrecting the promises that have been made to you. I asked the question earlier "where do ideas begin"? We think of begin as something we have to create. Ideas are never created; they are made known at their appointed time. Ideas are in work relation with your gifts. The more of your gift you use, the more ideas you will have.

Whenever I become so wrapped up in what gifts I have, living in purpose and walking in love, something reminds me of Jeremiah. God told Jeremiah "Before I formed you in the belly, I knew you". And then He told him where his gifts came from. "I had already made you a prophet before you were born (Jeremiah 1:5)". If He knew about Jeremiah and gave him his gifts and their assignment, before He was born, what does that say about you and me? So where do our ideas come from? They are already in place waiting on their appointed time to come forth. I have been asked if that was only for certain people. No!! Everyone in the earth's realm is impregnated with seed, time and harvest. It's how you use it that makes the difference. Usually in conversation the question would be asked, "then what's the difference between a believer in God and a non-believer". It's called intimacy. A believer walks within the guidelines of his or her faith in God. And within that walk you are entitled to certain blessings and promises. So, back to where we left off. Do we create the things we desire or do we resurrect them from creation? When I was born, all of my needs, desires, healing, wisdom, understanding, etc; were part of my creation. So whatever gifts I have or purpose I'm supposed to operate in, is already part of creation. When I talk about using faith to receive something that I can't see, it's because my spirit knows it's already part of God's creation. So with my faith and confession, I'm able to call forth/create from God's creation my earthly manifestations. That's my current level of experience that continues to get more and more interesting with time.

Life's purpose has already been commissioned. God is the author and finisher of all things. We are His creation and our purpose cannot be without His promises. For all things formed and unformed were created by God and part of a process to make us whole. Why was it necessary for the children of Israel to spend 40 years in the wilderness, or Joseph's life to be turned upside down before becoming second in command in Egypt? It was part of a preparation for change. Joseph's ordeal put him in the right place at the right time to interpret the dreams for the king of Egypt. The wilderness brought forth a people that were ready to stand on a promise to possess a land that was predestined to be theirs. We didn't know it but somewhere in our purpose, our path was designated to cross and the contents of these pages would be read. I could try to take the credit for meeting you, but that would be like me telling you I can fight your tomorrow's battle today. So we know whom the credit goes to.

The research, study and meditation that went into this project was the perfect opportune time for me to be taught. For the longest, I used to think that purpose was a thing about power. And I thought that power was determined by the size of your audience. I never gave the promise land trip that much thought until now. The revelation of an eleven-day trip taking 40 years was enlightening. In the past, I have tried to use logic, authenticity, and you name it, to understand the reason behind the 40 years. I've learned that God's multi-dimensional divine plan doesn't always make sense to my one-dimensional carnal mind.

Challenges

· · · · · ·

Challenges are those inevitable realities of life. Without their teaching, we would fall victim to circumstances. They are part of an assignment to precondition us against the attacks of the enemy. Challenges are a necessary element and one of the components of growth.

--Herman Hall

Chapter
2

CHALLENGES

We tend to think our greatest challenges were in our past failures. But much to our surprise, we learn that moving forward from our comfort zone requires much more effort than anything we may have experienced in the past. Though moving forward is rewarding (sowing seed and reaping a harvest), we must not be naive and be prepared to find ways to renew our strength, rekindle our spirit and rebuild our faith for the uncertainties and sometimes unpleasant conditions that lie ahead. We are not talking about conditions that are made by the enemy, but conditions that are caused by our own doing.

There is an old adage that says, if it doesn't kill you, it will make you stronger. It is in our darkest hour, when we are too weak to fight, that we understand the true meaning of being in the state of being, versus in the state of doing.

When you become seemingly separated from the very breath you breathe, you begin to realize that the true measure of a man is not what he or she does with their successes, but how well they handle their failures. It is precisely at this moment that you discover the true source for self-preservation, courage and perseverance. When a ship is at sea and ripped apart by the perfect storm, the crew are not known for their ability to overcome the storm. They are expected to endure storms because of their training. But they receive the recognition of heroism when they all chain themselves together (to save lives) and hold on to the only part of the ship that hasn't been destroyed, the foundation.

When life's storm becomes unbearable, remember the foundation. Remember you have the power to say to your storm, peace be still. With each victory over defeat, you send a clear message to life's storms that surrendering is not an option, and that you are a force to be reckoned with. The sweet smell of victory can bring you great joy but the journey and overwhelming odds you endure along the way are the real rewards.

Challenges put us through a process much like clay when it's in the potter's hands. After a daunting task of reshaping and refining, the potter places the item in the furnace as clay but removes it as ceramic ready to perform the function for which it was created. In the same manner, crisis helps to prepare us.

The critical commonality between clay and us is the fire. In simplistic terms, no fire (no refining) - (no challenges), no change. Metaphorically, both scenarios require the same process. In order to get rid of the impurities, the flaws and the blemishes, you must go through the refining process. Each time you emerge from the furnace (one of life's lessons), you find yourself back on course with life's purpose by the function you're able to perform. Greater depth of wisdom will emerge with you, creating balance and providing the inner strength needed to stand strong and stay the course. You will change those things you can and accept those things you have no control over. Wisdom will serve as your ornament of grace, a crown that will help you to manifest the desires of your heart.

Welcome challenges for they bring life's three major components: purpose, priority and process. They are the mechanism that brings about change. They are the catalyst that creates the enthusiasm that carries you to the highest point of excellence. If we could only adopt the attitude of the ant and be more proactive and less reactive; understanding that challenges are an inevitable reality of life. Anticipation and preparation are the best defense to combating challenges. Try reversing your thought process and accept that challenges come to build us up, not tear us down. Every challenge you encounter is an essential building block in reaching your divine purpose.

You cannot and will not operate in your divine purpose without challenges from the opposing forces. The opposing force, the Demonic stronghold, does not want you to achieve the greatness you were created to be. For our struggle is not against flesh and blood, but against the rulers, against the authorities, against the powers of darkness, and against the forces of evil in the earthly realms. But let not your heart be troubled because strong holds can be broken. They are not defeated by carnal weapon, but rather from divine might working from within. For it is with the inner strength of the heart that you find the courage to stay the course and face adversity.

Your inner strength will strategically navigate you through obstacles that will ultimately lead you to victory over any and every situation. Trials make us stronger; battles build our faith; and perseverance builds our character. Acknowledge and accept that each challenge is uniquely designed to make you stronger. Emerging from a challenge without the benefit of the lesson that it has come to teach is similar to the flight of a young fledgling, which leaves its nest too soon; obtaining neither the strength nor the balance to properly defend itself against its enemies.

Allow yourself to stay in the fold, stay in your rebuilding process until you have recovered from any wounds and are fully prepared to move forward. Study the reasoning that created your condition and start the repositioning process to avoid the same fate.

Continuing to meet the same fate diminishes faith and destroys the hope and confidence necessary to make dreams come true; the makings for the proverbial 'self fulfilling prophecy'. "For as a man thinketh in his heart, so is he (Proverbs 23:7, KJV)."

The tendency to distance ourselves from our troubles are common to all. This in itself could be the first mistake. During those times when you're confronted with troubles, remember that trouble is contrived from the condition you created by making a conscious decision to better yourself. It [trouble] is only here to honor your request and to help make your vision, your dream a reality. Ponder that thought for a moment; absorb the process and allow the concept to take hold. Learn to view your troubles as the 'chaos of change' that not only challenges you, but also creates the opportunity that moves you to the next level from where you are today. Trouble is a necessary element and component of growth. Without it, you would not be able to function.

That small cosmic nano second between mind and matter is where time stands still long enough, giving you the chance to affect the end result. Take that away and you take away your future. That space holds within it life's destiny. Embrace challenges, for they are only here to give us a chance to get it right. Getting it right gives us a second chance. They are merely the remnant of a well-worked decision whose time has come and gone. Their purpose is to nourish your mind with information and instructions for that new direction that will put you back on course with new expectations.

25

Your message to trouble should be that I will not surrender and become a victim of my circumstance, but rather my circumstance will become a victim of God's purpose and God's plan in my life. Proclaim no weapon formed against me will prosper. If you feel your situation is not favorable due to your faith, be encouraged by knowing that all things are working together for your good. Continue to sow good seed and expect a great harvest. Know that your true meaning for giving is not just to change a person's condition, but also to affect a person's destiny.

Stop undervaluing yourself. Undervaluing causes a false self-perception. The supreme purpose for this physical world that we live in is to enable us to experience life; learning how to be productive in different seasons; to overcome our challenges and to sow seed that bring forth good fruits. It brings to mind a season when the ultimate sacrifice was made, on a hill where the soil was made fertile through a sacrificial seed that fell upon the ground. And on the third day the grave and the ground was quicken; giving the world the greatest gift ever known to man.

So the next time life throws you one of its challenges, boldly step up and stare this trial in the face and say, "the seed has already been sown, the solution has already been put in place."

Vision and Empowerment

. . . . . .

There is an element of the mind

that's called the sensor. Sensors

are activated by vision. Having a

vision heightens your awareness,

putting your sensors on alert

for ways in making your

vision come true.

--Herman Hall

Chapter 3 | VISION AND EMPOWERMENT

D
o you know why, all of a sudden, there's so much talk about the law of attraction? It has to do with the power of visualization. All the time, we hear someone saying, "Visualize what you want." Have you ever wondered why that supposedly works? Or what's actually happening when you're visualizing something? Visualization heightens your awareness. When you visualize something, you activate your sensors. Sensory is part of your nerve fiber – the impulses that are being pasted to the central nervous system. It's an element of the brain that gives us the ability to detect, receive signals and motion and respond to them in a distinctive manner.

The distance a radio station can transmit and receive is determined by the amount of watts it emits. Our sensor acts as a receiver for us, transmitting and receiving information, but not by watts.

Our heightened awareness is not limited to just our immediate surrounding. We have the ability to sensor through the spirit by the spirit of God that lives in us. God is omnipresent – everywhere at the same time – making our distance of sensory unlimited. So what makes visualization so important is that we have the ability, through our spirit, to look worldwide for ways to make what we're visualizing come true.

When we hear the word vision, we immediately think of images, dreams, ideas, revelation, etc. What about feeling? Could vision and feeling be connected in any way? Have you ever visualized something that brought a smile to your face? Like the last time you were with the love of your life. Or maybe that vacation cruise or some other nice vacation you were on. Did you know that when you smile your energy level rises? Even though your energy may only be brief, according to physic, it has to rise in order to smile. But notice there doesn't have to be any physical changes to the outward appearances.

Let's take it a step further - vision creates empowerment. If you are having a good feeling, irrespective to whom or where it's from, doesn't it usually bring about a smile? The feeling could perhaps come from external vision or internal mental imagery. Did you know that the state of empowerment is generated from feeling and/or emotion?

That's the power, the law and principles of visualization. Start focusing your attention on something and you will begin to receive ways to make it happen.

There's information out there – good and bad – that will give insight to what you're thinking about. Your job is to keep your thoughts and vision moral and honest. The information you receive is just information. How you use and act upon the information will determine the degree or type of reward you receive.

According to science, before we can do anything, we first have to be empowered (given the authorization) from the brain to proceed. I initiate these thoughts on vision and empowerment because of their importance to living life to its full potential and there are no universal written standards to living to your full potential. The only standard that exists is the one you created to fulfill your goals. Living life to its full potential is done through a request that's made only by you. His or her level of request determines each person's success or potential.

Vision can serve as a two-edged sword. It can be a mood maker as well as a mood breaker. Most of the time, our mood is more of how someone feels about us than how we feel about ourselves. If that's your self-perception, you are headed for an emotional crash. The way you feel about yourself determines how you feel about the world around you. If you start your day with an inferiority complex, you are defeated before you get started. You would have been better off staying in bed. People will see you based on how you see yourself. If you want a good reflection as to how people see you, just look at how you see yourself.

Because you emanate certain messages, and certain impulses come through your self-perception, that controls how other people perceive you. Self-empowerment is not what occurs on the outside, but what happens on the inside.

Start your day with confidence, boldness and a clear perception of who you are. If you start your day with a distorted vision of who you are, it will cause you to see yourself in a diminished perspective, while seeing your challenges in an over inflated perspective. A mediocre vision will, at best, produce a mediocre result. Get excited about who you are. And get a visual of the earth celebrating with you while it's spinning on its axis. As your mind thinketh, so are you. Allow yourself to meditate on the desires of your heart as though they exist. Many of us are living today on yesterday's lifeline. You can't change what happened in the past by refusing to live in the present. But we can let what happened in the past teach us how to have a better future. We should be showing progress in the way we respond to things. Today's situation should not be getting yesterday's response. You can't create a future if you're not able to move beyond your past.

We live in a time where there is excessive compulsiveness to continue to hurt someone that may have hurt us. Some of this is due to how fragmented our vision has become. Somehow we have to re-gather the pieces and become whole again before we completely self-destruct. A distorted, fragmented vision is the culprit for most dismantled relationships.

It's amazing how a distorted vision in a relationship can cause the 80 percent you're getting from your mate look smaller than the 20 percent you're not getting. Vision can become distorted to a point it causes you to lose your way. It will impair you in such a way that you can easily be deceived.

The eyes are the windows to the heart and your heart holds your most valuable treasure. Over 80 percent of what we learn comes through the eyes. Raising your expectation and broadening your vision may help minimize those things that keep taking you places but getting you nowhere. We cannot continue with things that are making big promises but have a track record of making small deliveries. They are little nuances that take your attention from the more important things. Ladies, have you ever attempted to go grocery shopping but before you could get out of the house, your girlfriend calls? She's in the area and wants to stop by for a few minutes. A few minutes turns into a couple of hours. Then there goes the time for grocery shopping. Self-empowerment's main purpose is staying productive. Operating in your purpose makes it easy to tell your friends or your sibling that you have a few errands to run and will get back with them later.

Self-empowered people are not known for a lot of nonproductive down time; they are known for their time management skills. They are more the quality assessment type that is constantly doing checks and balances and they are very selective of the company they keep.

They will quickly point out that they believe the company you keep can sometime determine what kind of vision you have. If everyone in your circle is looking to you for answers, you might need to change your circle. Your circle of people needs to inspire you, cause you to study harder, intimidate you at times, and make you grow.

The time has come for you to empower yourself with the power of visualization and pursuit of happiness. Understand that the thing you hate the most is sometimes the thing you are most gifted in. The fact that you dislike something because of its imperfection could mean you are gifted in that area. How else would you know a change is needed? An elevated vision could be an illustration of an undiscovered talent. Having the capability to correct a problem is a window of opportunity. Certain creation can only be seen and understood by its creator. This could be the first glimpse of evidence of an undiscovered gift.

Vision is the lifeline of the mind. The mind without a vision is like the body without nourishment; it loses its physical attribute you need to sustain life. Where there's no vision, people perish. Your mechanism of social control is affected by your vision. Vision is the first step to manifestation. It gives the body authority or permission to put in motion an act of reality.

One of the biggest problems we have when it comes to vision is the level we visualize on. If your goals are not aimed high enough, then what happens to things above your goals?

We know that everything beneath your goals is done subsequently in the process of getting to your goals. But what about those things you need for life's satisfaction that's above where you have your goals set? I say this to say that too many times, we have a single-minded vision. Meaning if your goal or vision is just to make more money or live in a nice home, what about health? What about a good family relationship or a good educational foundation to work from? Too many times, we reach our goal but do not achieve self-actualization. Money and homes, in many cases, only gives the appearance of happiness. Physical things can only satisfy physical needs. We are more than just physical.

Total wholeness stretches across multiple boundaries. It covers the physical level, as well as the spiritual level. Your sole purpose for existence is to fulfill your vision with the gifts and talents that's been placed in you. Your vision is part of a larger theater that's in creation. You and I are one of the segmented pieces of a greater plan. That's why we come with specific skills, attributes and craftsmanship. They are part of an operating system that we use in our purpose. Many times we struggle with our passion and our purpose. But just remember, it's not always the one that starts the race who is the one to finish, just as a cup of water shouldn't be measured by the size of the cup when it has an unlimited water source. The same goes with us. We are vessels operating with an unlimited power from a never-ending source.

How to Manifest Your Vision

Write your vision down, as best as possible. Then make a list of the things your vision will either have an impact on, or the things your vision will achieve. Now, get it in your spirit by verbalizing what you just wrote. Here is something not to do. Don't limit the success of your vision to only what you know. Because God is too powerful and too masterful for you to understand how He's going to manifest your vision. Here is something for thought that I do every day with my vision. I make the statement that the manifestation of my vision better positions me to live out my purpose. And every day my purpose is walking in love and adding value to others' lives whether it's health, wealth, wisdom or whatever. That's a personal revelation that I've received to help nurture my vision of manifestation.

Develop an attitude that all of your needs are met; think of it and verbalize it as often as you can. In doing this, you're sending out an invitation. You are inviting the laws and principles into your life to make that happen. The words that we speak release a call to create. When the call is made, the process of manifestation begins in the spiritual realm. When we get this revelation, we then will understand that we are part of a never-ending source. If we are connected to an all powerful, all knowing source, then God the Source knew that this day, at this time we would be doing exactly what we are doing. And it's probably safe to say that God knows about our beginning and ending in this physical realm. This is a vision of empowerment.

Knowing this information doesn't minimize the human physical side of us, but it does help to put in perspective who is in subjection to whom. It is comforting to know that my spirit is making intercession with God for my needs. Scholars will tell you that your spirit has memory of your future that your mind struggles to understand. If we are part spirit, and we are, then the spirit will lead us to make the type of decision that will fulfill God's plan.

The enemy is always out to confuse the plan and destroy your hope. Because he knows if he can destroy your hope, he can cause you to lose sight of your future. And if you lose sight of your future, then God's plan for you would never be fulfilled. Here's something to always keep in mind. Regardless of where you are or where you have been, God's original plan for your life is still His final intention. That's not going to change. You can't make a mess too big that He doesn't already have a solution for. There are no paths that God can't work into His plan. Some paths are more difficult and require more work than others. If you want God's favor, then stay in God's purpose. If you stay in God's purpose, you're in covenant to receive God's promises. God never gives vision where He hasn't already made provision. Your physical needs will always be met as long as your intention is to elevate your spiritual growth. When you are satisfying your spiritual needs, you are operating within your highest physical form.

Personal Growth

· · · · · ·

Personal growth is essential for overcoming setbacks and sacrifices. Many times a small adjustment in attitude can amount to a significant move in altitude. Personal growth is all about learning how to increase self-worth without sacrificing self-respect.

--Herman Hall

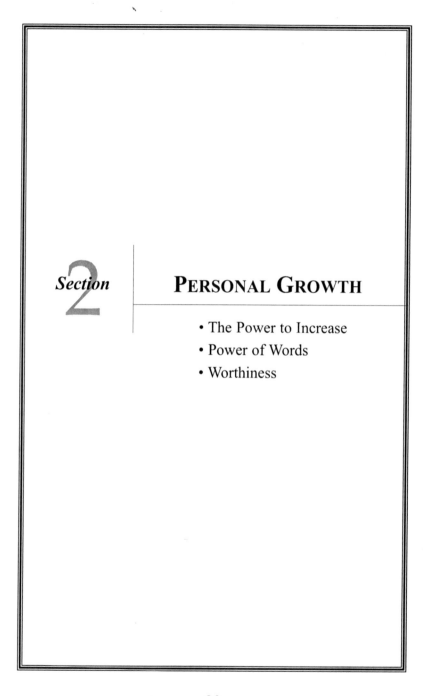

Section 2 | # PERSONAL GROWTH

- The Power to Increase
- Power of Words
- Worthiness

The Power To Increase

. . . . . .

The power to increase is about coming into alignment with your opportunity. Understanding the laws and order needed to carry that opportunity to fulfillment.

--Herman Hall

<table>
<tr><td>*Chapter* 4</td><td>THE POWER TO INCREASE</td></tr>
</table>

Normally when we hear the word increase, we think of money, wealth and material possessions. That's because we are programmed to think that way. But increase is more than just money. There is increase in wisdom and increase in understanding. Increase in discipline and increase in health. Personally, the most important thing I would want to have is an increase in good health. There are many with wealth today who would be willing to trade places for good health.

In my early years, my experience with money was not being disciplined enough to manage it. Finally, with a little maturity, I was able to prioritize using my finances with the help of both wisdom and discipline. Wisdom and its usage were my first steps to controlling my increase. I soon learned how to apply those same techniques for managing challenging situations in my everyday life.

Now it's about time we stepped up, using that power and executing our authority to reclaim what's already been predestined for us. In some cases, we have allowed ambition and pride to hold us hostage. When we get so ambitious that we can no longer free ourselves to enjoy the simpler things in life, we begin to slowly close that value which connects us to our source. What started out as a good thing slowly turns into something unhealthy. Would you shut oxygen off from the brain while working on an important assignment? No way!! We must be aware and not interfere with those things that empower us. The power to increase, as you will see, is more about harmony - being of one mind.

Many of us are looking for a way to be in harmony or be in purpose. We think being in purpose is being in power. I'm often told (in conversation) by others that they don't know what their purpose in life is, indicating that this is affecting their power to increase. First, stop looking for your purpose and find your passion. In most cases (if not already), your passion will lead you to your purpose. Who's to say you're not already operating in your purpose? Can a tree say "I'm not a tree because I'm not part of the forest?" Is it safe to say that the sun is not shining anyplace because we can't see it? Every day we have an opportunity to be in our purpose by being and operating in love. But we look for purpose in all the wrong places. Purpose is about serving. Purposefully serving others (in some way) with love. Love conquers all. Every good deed you do and every kind word you say is part of your purpose.

Love is the first discipline of The Power To Increase. Operating in love puts you in solidarity with the universal and divine force of nature. It's the unanimity of the mind, being in oneness with everyone in your space, that gives you the opportunity to purposefully show love. Every time you seize the moment to show love, your purpose expands. Remember your purpose is not all about having an impact on thousands of people's lives; it's more about impacting your life. If you did ten kind things today to ten different people, who's mostly affected? Would it be the ten individuals or would it be you? You would benefit the most. Because each person you spoke to was an opportunity to improve what you were speaking about. After each person, you gain a better understanding of what you were doing.

A growth in wisdom is a fulfillment of purpose and The Power To Increase is under your control. Your increase is already woven into the tapestry of 'who you are' and programmed inside the system you operate from. The operative word is "already". That's why it's so important to have a clear vision of what you are doing. Write it down if necessary. A written plan is more likely to be carried out than a conceptualized one. Over 70 percent of what you do is a reflection of what you see. Perhaps that's where we get the phrase, "where there's no vision, one perishes". Your vision has unlimited access to infinite resources. You get to decide where you want to be in life. Your mind literally becomes a magnet for information, drawing from every known intelligence source.

Each time you share (unbeknownst to you), there is an evaluation of perfection going on. For example, the faster I conclude the writing for this book, the faster new information tries to come in. There are times when information is coming in so fast that my writing is no longer coming from me, but rather coming through me. It is during this time that I'm writing beyond my comprehension. Remember earlier we said that each time we share information, we empower ourselves. The resources that we are mentally connected to evaluate everything that we do. Every experience we have ever had, every person we have talked to and each book we have read becomes a reservoir of information. Every observation you make, every suggestion you take and all of your self-evaluations are extracts from your supply storage. These are universal laws and principles in operation designed to give you and me The Power To Increase.

In other parts of the book I talk about "...going within". Everything you need is already in place in seed form. Seed form meaning the source is in place to give resource to all your needs. Those unknown desires you have are nothing more than resources being birthed into purpose. We are part of God's resource carrying within us God the source. Therefore whatsoever we ask, believing God, the source, that we have received, will be given to us. As you begin to develop, your resources in the form of gifts and talents find their places to fulfill your purpose. We are part of a much bigger plan. We are intended for increase in every area of our being. The subtitle of the book says, "giving birth to a life without limits".

44

When we are in alignment with God our source, we don't have limits. Operating in the order of God's laws and principles makes us co-create with God, giving birth to life without limits. Think of it this way... If you're not being effective in what you're doing, be willing to slow it down and see what order you're in. Then ask yourself, 'If everything is a major challenge for me, I may be trying to nurture a gift that has no seed form. Could I be trying to nurture someone else's seed?' Step away from it and think about it again. If a plan is not working for me, could it be because it doesn't belong to me? Is it possible I have desired or adopted someone else's plan? An idea is not successful because of what you can do for it. An idea or plan can only succeed when it tells you what to do with it. Remember an idea is part of your resource working for your purpose. Be sure you're not trying to give birth to someone else's dream. If it seems as if you are in this type of trench, relinquish any ownership you have of it. If it drifts away from you, then it's not being harvested through you, it's being harvested by you. Your seed can only become your harvest in your field. It will not drift nor be delayed. Harvesting seeds other than your own requires significantly more effort with no reliable assurance.

The Power To Increase is in your hand. Too many times we opt not to increase; settling for far less than what's actually meant for us to have. And many times, that's because we don't want to come out of our comfort zone. To be positioned for an increase should never feel like a major displacement. A feeling of displacement could be the sign of trying to make a transition happen before its time.

Many times, we want to move from one phase in life before all of the lessons in the current phase are learned. If you're trying to move ahead of a crowd and there's no place to go, all you do is frustrate yourself and anger those around you who may be placed there to help. The same is true when trying to move ahead without preparing yourself. You keep repeating the process and, often, the inherent and invisible mistakes.

There is one important fact to remember--nothing just arbitrarily happens. Everything has an order in which it is done. The power to increase is about synchronicity: aligning yourself with the order of your purpose. The ego doesn't like order. Its mode of operation is not to keep us in alignment. The ego is self-based, motivated by an excessive or exaggerated sense of self-importance. It has no regard for goals or dreams. It treats them like foreign objects. Why? Because the ego has a self-centered, egocentric nature. It would rather use temporary fixes instead of permanent solutions. You will find that the ego is most active in the absence of guidelines or protocols. So you can resolve the ego interference simply by re-applying laws and principles. As we said earlier, increase comes in forms other than money.

We are the product of a plan designed to create from within itself. We co-exist our own existence; meaning through your intent, you have created who you are. Everything about you is designed to procreate itself. It was the part of creation that you inherited. We are the offspring of a more highly complex master plan.

Look at Moses in the wilderness. When the time came for the children of Israel to increase, God spoke to Moses. He said "it's time to get out of here. You have been circling around this mountain long enough." We all know the story of Moses and the children of Israel well. That journey from Egypt to the Promise Land was less than a one-week long trip. So what took them so long? "Where there is no vision the people perish". The Promise Land was too good to be true. They couldn't see themselves worthy. They were letting their condition identify who they were. At one time or another, we've all been there. Even though they had been delivered from Egypt, they were never set free of bondage. Even though physically they were no longer in Egypt, they were mentally still held hostage by a slave mentality. So the Promise Land was never part of their vision. It took the younger generation, born in the wilderness, to see their way to the Promise Land. The one thing the people in the wilderness never realized was that they were part of a bigger plan. They limited themselves to what they had.

If you don't have a vision, create one and meditate on it at leisure. You become this magnetic energy force sending and receiving like-minded signals. Bring yourself in alignment with God's divine order; building your faith and perfecting your character. Refuse to be distracted, reject and decline imperfection; mingle with those that have your answer; and limit yourself to those who have your problem. You have the power to increase; you have the power to gain true prosperity.

Meditation

One of the most overlooked processes in bringing us in alignment with our powers within is meditation. Meditation has been around since the beginning of time. Many forms and styles have been created just for the sake of marketing. There is nothing complicated about meditation; it is simply having a quiet moment alone with you and your thoughts. It's a way to stimulate the brain, which in return causes changes in your cognition and in your emotions. Many years ago (except in the business community), meditation was not popular in the secular society. But it has since gained more notoriety in the more popular culture. Doctors at the Mind-Body Medical Institute (http://en.wikipedia.org/wiki/Meditation) report that clinical trials have confirmed that heart disease can be reversed with a comprehensive program that includes meditation. The report goes on to say that your metabolism, heart rate, respiration, blood pressure, and brain chemistry can all be changed through the use of meditation.

Meditation is a process of quieting down the mind and moving into a higher level of consciousness. This is the level frequently visited to meditate on the things you want manifested in your life. This is where you will have an encounter with divine wisdom, laws and principles to begin the process of putting your priorities in order. The whole premise behind meditation is to go within for strength and guidance. Fitness centers across the country are adding meditation classes. The corporate industries are getting more involved with meditation in the workplace.

Many of your religious organizations practice meditation during their services. Whatever your profession or passion in life is, adding meditation gives you that competitive edge. Whenever you bring the mind, body and spirit together, and create that balance between thoughts, awareness and well-being, balance will help to bring spiritual and physical healing to multiple levels.

Before You Meditate

In order to get the maximum benefit from meditation, you need to be in the right mindset. Meditation promotes discipline, which causes you to raise your expectation of yourself. But before that can happen, you have to remove any form of negative emotion or negative judgment. During meditation, always focus on the solution, never on the desire. Continuing to focus on your desires will obstruct you from seeing your solution. If all you're looking at is the problem, you will never see the answer. Meditation will help improve your navigational skills to keep you in line with life's destiny. Keep an open mind, for the creator of the universe knew far in advance what you would have need of.

The Results of Meditation

Over time, you will notice a shift in your awareness and in your desires. The things you once struggled with will become part of a lifestyle change. Change of events will have a huge gravitational pull in bringing together your new priorities and your new levels of understanding. It will seem like a world inside of a world opening up to remove those self-imposed limitations that stand between you and your desires.

49

You will notice a remarkable difference in stress and anxiety. The rewards never end. New levels of awareness continue to improve and bring new ways of life.

I recorded a meditation CD called First Step to Meditation. If you're new to meditation, the CD is a good foundational starting point. If this is something you feel might be of help, email me and I will see what I can do to get you a copy.

Financial

The power to increase extends itself to managing our finance. Prosperity is not all about what God can give us; it also includes how well we manage/invest what we already have.

Let me briefly share a few money management tips with you. The area we seem to lack in is our retirement. Some of us don't know that our retirement plans are affected by the world economical conditions. In March of 2009, our market experienced a 12-year low. Many retirement accounts were drastically reduced to as much as 40 percent. After further review, we have learned that some of the losses could have been avoided. A lot of losses were attributed to portfolios exposed to too much risk. If you don't understand the risk balancing formula, then do the next best thing-- keep your risk tolerance to a minimum. Retirement plans were not created as an investment tool. They were for tax deferment and to participate in an employee percentage-matching program. Unless you have been skillfully trained in the stock exchange money markets, leave the investing to the expert on Wall Street.

Throughout the Bible, we see that God has a lot to say about finances. The power to increase is keeping God involved in your finances. Understanding and observing certain basic principles will keep you from letting greed be your only motive for prosperity. Having abundance is part of God's plan for us but we must not forget that giving and being a blessing to others is part of the spiritual law.

Solomon understood the principles of prosperity. He was one of the richest men who ever lived. His writing revealed many truths regarding finances.

> "Honor the Lord with thy substance, and with the first fruits of all thine increase: so thy barns be filled with plenty, and thy presses shall burst forth with new wine." (Proverbs 3:9-10, AMP)

True riches is about a pure motive and a pure heart to establish God's covenant by extending your blessing to others. Financial defeat is not always because of what we're not doing; sometimes it's because of what we are doing. What we believe and speak affects the increases in our life. The very thing that was created to bring increase to us, our words, are sometimes the thing that works against us the most. Our words are the last thing from us to go to work for us. What are we putting our words to work doing? Are they working on poverty or prosperity, sickness or health? Readjust your financial thoughts to become more a liability breaker and an asset maker.

Power of Words

• • • • • •

Words either add value or take value away. There are no in betweens. Words will always be a reflection of where you have been and where you're going.

--Herman Hall

Chapter 5 | **POWER OF WORDS**

❝ ❝ Let the words of my mouth, and the meditation of my heart, be acceptable in thy sight" (Psalms 19:14, KJV).

You are about to see how important it is to be careful with words. The words we use distinguish the difference between giving power to and/or taking power from. Words can bring life and words can take life away. Your confidence, insecurities, ambition, weakness and strength all lie within the power of your words.

"Death and life are in the power of the tongue..." (Proverb 18:21, KJV)

Words have such a proverbial effect because we view them as a reflection of our values.

Whenever a person's principle has been violated and their character misrepresented, they become defensive to protect the one thing they have left--their self-worth. Once your self-worth is damaged, the process to restore it can be long and difficult. Words are used as a means of communication and to collect insightful information to make decisions. Whenever we speak and are being spoken to (whether it's true or false), our first reaction is to perceive the information to be factual. The first second of receiving information is your most vulnerable moments. Credibility and perception are immediately assessed. You will automatically browse through a frame of reference regarding the person who's doing the speaking for their credibility. All of this happens within the first few seconds after being spoken to. Why do you think TV ads always say "you have to respond to this offer within the next half hour to receive this special offer"? But yet you will hear that same ad hours, even days, later saying the same thing. The advertisers know that if they can't get you to respond within the first few minutes, chances are you will not. Why is that so? A thirty second TV ad can't provide enough information for the brain to hold onto for a long period of time. Even in our infancy, words from those around us helped to form our sense of self. Our growth and course of action was formed on the type of communication we received. As an infant, we were conditioned to believe that words could always be believed and trusted. Because of this conditioning, there are times when we find ourselves wanting to believe someone, knowing that they are not being truthful. Which tells us we are creatures of habit.

If we hear something repetitively, we tend to convince ourselves it must be the truth. That was established when we were babies growing up and the only thing we had and depended on was words. Why do you think you are told to never use the words, "I can't", but instead use the words, "I can". Words have creative power. If you believe you can, a transformation will takes place. The very thing you professed with the intent to receive becomes a reality. We are co-creators with the spiritual law. We speak a natural thing into existence by the use of the spiritual law. The earth (and everything in it) operates on spiritual laws. God the spirit spoke it into existence. So as long as we are speaking within the spirit laws, we are co-creators in the spirit with God. How fitting for the bible to be called the Word.

"In the beginning was the Word, and the Word was with God, and the Word was God" (John 1:1, KJV)

Words have more transformation of power than we realize. We know the story well concerning the birth of Jesus. How the transformation of power to Mary was given from an angel. The angle only brought the word. Mary then believed the word and she was with the word and the word was made flesh.

"And the Word was made flesh, and dwelt among us, and we beheld his glory, the glory as of the only begotten of the Father,) full of grace and truth." (John 1:14, KJV)

Now you know why I started this subject with the phrase, "Let the words of my mouth and the meditation of my heart be acceptable". Words have their way of giving and receiving, building and tearing down. Words can empower you and words can dismember you. Embedded in words are all the ingredients of life, health, love, abundance, prosperity, wisdom and understanding. The more words you subject yourself to, the more reassured you are. Performance comes easy when you have done adequate preparation. How can you recall from memory that which has never been stored? Let's talk a little bit about how important it is to speak the word. As strange as it might sound, there are people who are doers of things that they don't even believe in. Now the problem I have with that is how effective are you in something you don't believe in? Jesus said to Peter, "Peter I know you have been following me around and learning from my teaching and you have told me who others say I am, but who do you say I am?"

> "He saith unto them, But who say ye that I am?
> And Simon Peter answered and said, Thou art the
> Christ, the Son of the living God." (Matthew 16:15-
> 16, KJV)

Why did he ask Peter that knowing what he was going to say? Because He knows it's from the heart that a man speaks. He knew that Peter would empower himself through the confession of his mouth. And He also knew that this would give Him the opportunity to tell Peter that flesh and blood did not reveal this to him.

56

And Jesus answered and said unto him, Blessed art thou Simon Bar-jo –na: for flesh and blood hath not revealed it unto thee, but my Father which is in heaven." (Matthew 16:17, KJV)

Jesus needed to sow those words as seeds into Peter so he could reap their harvest later during his ministry. Why was sowing this seed so important? Because Jesus knew of the trials that Peter would face in his ministry and that this word in his heart would be there to provide comfort during those times.

When you need to be encouraged, you have to speak from the heart. Words of inspiration from friends are good but their words don't carry the seed of life. Words of life are words that have already been planted in you and have had time to take root, develop and are now ready to bear fruit. Later in life, Peter was able to overcome his challenges because of the words Jesus had sown in him. He had already informed Peter of what was to happen. And Peter had witnessed many acts of wonders that were performed by Jesus, which later became his support system. When we are using words to claim victory, on what foundation are we proclaiming it? What victory platform are we standing on? What challenge have we overcome to be able to use as a frame of reference? Understand that words can esteem themselves above any social structure, above any condition, position or arduous task. They guide and navigate us from within. No wonder Jesus told Peter "flesh and blood has not revealed this to you".

Peter was having a divine moment, much the same way we do, but on a level that we can decipher its meaning. Remember when you would come home from school and your parent would ask, "what did you learn today" and you really wanted to say "nothing". Well, technically if the information you received at school could not be processed and put into a workable plan, then to say "I learned nothing" would have been correct. Let's illustrate using a free ninety-minute seminar. Statistics show that the average person who attends a free ninety-minute seminar will, in 48 hours, forget eighty percent of what they heard. Why? Because you can't remember what you haven't received. The operational plan, the process, is what's taught during the course. If you opt not to pay for the course, then the ninety-minute seminar is nothing more than fragmented information that never got processed. Information that never gets processed is like a seed that never got planted; it dies, it vanishes, it disintegrates. God works in a similar fashion by giving us the end result of His expected plan. Except for one major difference. He gives us the complete course. Complete course meaning He gives us what He expects but He also includes all the warning signs along the way. With every disappointment, He's there to give restoration. In every difficulty, He's lending a helping hand. A ninety-minute seminar can only give hope and possibilities. But just one moment of favor from God will create life-changing opportunities. Whenever you believe in His word, that word begins to take on a life form. Noah was told to build a ship because it was going to rain. Those very words "build a ship" took life form.

All of the engineering skills that were needed to build that boat were now operating within those words. They were just waiting for Noah to believe and accept them so they could carry out their assignment. Once accepted, they moved in and became one with Noah, bringing to his remembrance everything he had need of to complete the job. Why is it that belief and acceptance are so important? Without them, the seed of life never gets sown and the gifts of life are never manifested. It is your faith, your belief and your acceptance that produces the fertilization and provides the umbilical cord that the seed needs to live out its life expectancy. Words and their creative power will be here for the duration of time. Get in the habit of speaking them over you, preferably first thing in the morning. Bind those things that keep you going in circles. Remove their power of influence from around you. Tell your situation just as God told the children of Israel "it's time for a change. I have been here long enough".

> "Ye have compassed this mountain long enough:
> turn you northward." (Deuteronomy 2:3, KJV)

Why do we accept the shadows of mediocrity when we have been given a life of abundance? Speak to your sickness, scarcity, lack and shortage. Poverty has no place with you. Speak those things that are not as though they were. Let's make it personal. This is the day that the Lord has given me and I will receive, build and prosper in it. Now I have spoken, so shall it be.

Worthiness

• • • • • •

A house divided against itself
cannot stand. I surrender who I'm
trying to be to come in alignment
with who I am.

--Herman Hall

Chapter 6

WORTHINESS

Closing the Trench

Trenches, as we know them, are referred to as openings; as cuts in the ground; a ditch. Dugouts and channels that expose themselves to the elements but also can be used to protect. But let's explore a type of trench that has nothing to do with the environmental elements, but rather with the working of the mind.

The subtitle of this book, Giving Birth to a Life Without Limits, has been one of the most inspired moments of my life. Inspirational writing is one of the ways I can reach out and be of service to others. In this session, we will begin to see how we unintentionally leave gaps and holes with family and friends that can easily, and often too quickly, get filled with wrong information and misinterpreted perception.

In the next few minutes, I will share with you a way in which you can change your life and the lives of others that you share a relationship with. A relationship is anyone that's frequently in your space that you communicate with on a regular basis. After this session, you will be empowered to help change the lives of those around you. Many of us are in a position to use our influence to help others control certain behavior. But there are two areas that deeply affect the human spirit that so often go unnoticed. They are unity and accountability. For example, let's use spouses and significant others. When men correct the children in a home setting, they normally handle it this way. "Your mother is going to whip you for junking up her house!" Did you say her house!! Normally, when women correct the children in a car setting they usually say, "…your father is going to get you for junking up his car". His car!! What about when men say, "you are NEVER ready on time". Or when women say, "you ALWAYS do the same thing with your clothes; can't you for ONCE in your life do something different like hang them up?" Sound familiar??

Now to get the most from this analogy, let's use the same attitude in a more personal experience. I used the children and clothes in this example but modify it to make it meaningful for you. I think we already see what's wrong with this picture. How can you improve this situation? Let's start with the first situation. When you say things like "your mother's house" or "your father's car", where is your ownership; where is the unity?

Are you not also accountable? Anything started as a joint venture, as in this example of a family correctional setting, should be addressed as a joined voice. Remember in the beginning I mentioned misinterpreted perception, that which is explained or understood incorrectly. What message do you think the children are getting? They are probably saying it's ok to junk up the car as long as dad's not around. Is that really the way you want them to feel? Maybe there are certain things they shouldn't do in the car at all. You don't want to give them an incorrect understanding of something that they shouldn't be doing. If they happen to spill something and stain the upholstery, now the responsibility shifts. Now it's no longer the responsibility of the children to answer but the responsibility is now on you to answer why they were allowed to have liquid in the car in the first place. Same thing goes for the house. If they are junking up the house, the message should be "clean up this stuff now". Because God forbid if they break something and you have to explain why they were playing in that area.

Let's remove the car and the house from the scenario. How about an agreement you made with each other about a certain way you will conduct yourselves around others. What happens when that's not honored? Some way you find out that their word is only good as long as they are in your presence. There goes trust; trust begins to break down. Whenever we fail to speak with one voice or live in oneness, our area of responsibility is infected by a cavity. Cavity meaning our commitment now has a flaw and becomes subject to further decay if unattended. That nano second flaw creates a space.

That space, if not closed, in time, can erode into a gap the size of a canyon. And wherever erosion occurs, be it land or trust, no new growth can be expected until the condition that's causing the problem has been removed. Stop the erosion and the separation by bringing back the oneness and speaking with one voice.

Another area where we can seek improvement is with the words we use; words such as always, never or can't. What are we really saying? Are we deliberately sending a message here? When you say to someone, they never get it right or they always think they know everything. Do you know what they are processing? Do you fully understand the impact your words may have on them? Their mind is saying undeserving, not good enough, worthless. In other words, their self worth is going south fast. You probably don't mean to come across that way, but that's what's happening on the inside of the other person, in the trenches of their mind. You can be the judge by recalling an incident from your past and the way you were made to feel. If you tell me I always do it wrong or backwards, you are 'killing off' my spirit, thwarting my ambitions; you are undermining my self worth. Even though it's done in small micro ways, nevertheless, it's still being torn down. Over time, I will begin to translate that into not being worthy enough.

Sometimes, we feel it takes those types of behavior in order to get anything done. Then to take away the guilt of what we're doing, we try to rationalize it as 'motivating' vs the 'goading' that it truly is. What you are doing is getting short-term results but creating long-term problems.

You're never going to see change by pointing out faults in others. The core of who you are and the way you want to feel starts in you. You are the change that your situation needs. You are the teacher and more is taught by what you do than by what you say. Do you know why a machine works so well? It's because all the parts are working for the same cause. They only have one agenda and that is to work together. You see, the parts on the machine understand that unless they are one hundred percent committed to working together as one, the finished product will be flawed and will have to be done over. If you love someone, they should know it by the way you make them feel. Sometimes words have to be used when feeling is not speaking loud enough.

Spiritual Growth

. . . . . .

Spiritual growth is realigning your

purpose to the order and structure

of God -- serving at the highest

call by making contributions that

add value to the lives of others.

--Herman Hall

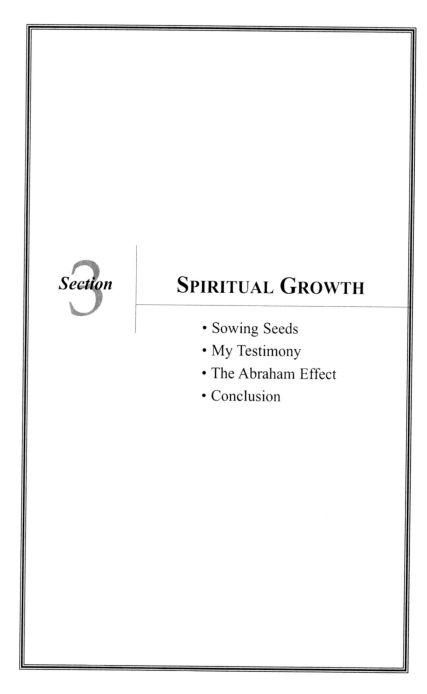

Section 3

SPIRITUAL GROWTH

- Sowing Seeds
- My Testimony
- The Abraham Effect
- Conclusion

Sowing Seeds

• • • • • •

My seed takes care of my need.

Make every day your intention to

add value to someone else's life.

Because in doing so you

change your own.

--Herman Hall

Chapter **7** | SOWING SEEDS

T here are so many different individual views on sowing seeds.

During my adolescent years, my perception of good deeds had to do with doing for others and putting money in the offering plate. I can vividly recall the words during the offering service were "God loves a cheerful giver." Today it has gotten to the point that you can't turn on a TV or a radio without hearing someone talk about God loving a cheerful giver. As in anything, the scammers and the imitators caught on to this and found a way to take a good thing and use it for greed.

I want to share a few incidences I have experienced and then get your view. One day, I was downtown and this lady was very distraught over not having enough money to get her car out of pay parking.

She couldn't pay the parking attendant for her car because the ATM machine was broken and she didn't have enough cash on hand. After inquiring what was wrong and discovering she only needed a few dollars, I provided the amount needed. My question is, "would that be considered the same as give and it shall be given to you?" Let's try another one. During a paralyzing snowstorm, I approached a broken down motorist whose car was buried in the snow. Fortunately, I was able to drive around the snow buried car because my vehicle was a four-wheel drive. I witnessed this motorist trying to dig his car out without a shovel. After a brief conversation with him, I went home, got my shovel and returned to help the motorist dig the car out. Again, is this one of those give and receive deeds? The last incident I want to share is the time I was in a grocery store and two customers were checking out at the cash register but realized they were short on cash to pay for the items. From the conversation the customers were having with the cashier, I could tell they needed to keep all of the items and therefore couldn't decide which items to put back. So I nodded to the cashier that I would take care of the difference. And, of course, the customers graciously thanked me. Again I ask, "is this what is meant about give and it shall be given to you?" Was I being a cheerful giver, or was I just doing what any average person would do in this type of situation?

So what is doing good deeds or sowing seeds? Many feel that an act of kindness will be met by another act of kindness. When this doesn't happen, our faith becomes overshadowed with doubt and what we thought was true seems to just be a big misunderstanding.

Could it be that the reward is being able to give? I raise the question because of some of the conversations I've had recently. There are those that only give because of what they expect to receive. But what I find interesting is if you ask them what they are expecting to receive back, they have no answer. It concerns me when I hear people teaching that you only have to have faith in God to be ensured success or that a certain amount of offering will guarantee a blessing. In reality, it takes a combination of faith and works, trial and error, success and struggle to produce the kind of success we want. Confessing with your mouth and believing in your heart are the first steps. Then there will come the means in which the manifestation will take place.

Each time we participate in giving, we are given the opportunity to receive. Not the kind of reception that brings about material things, but the kind that brings wisdom to teach us the ultimate purpose of giving. You can give of yourself or you can give of your possessions. Giving of your possessions usually is a response to a need. Giving of yourself, in many cases, is a response to destiny. How do we affect someone's destiny? We affect their destiny when they are in need of a friend, sharing wisdom, giving words of encouragement, standing in the gap or interceding in prayer for their needs. It brings joy to our heart to help satisfy a need, and it brings completeness to our purpose to assist in someone's destiny. The giving of love, prayer, and material things opens the door for us to experience a higher awareness for ourselves and help to bring new meaning to someone else's life. You will transcend to levels that you won't have words to explain.

Many of us are sowing seeds but are not reaping what we sow, or are we? How many times have we been wrong about what we thought we should be receiving? When you sow unconditionally, you receive unconditionally. Remember the old saying, "You reap what you sow?" That cliché has a lot more meaning than we realize. Yes, the one that receives does benefit, but good deeds are not always done just for the benefit. We won't go into that here. Before a seed can be sown, that seed must first go through a period of nurturing and cultivating. We always refer to the seed concept as seed, time and harvest. That may be the case in the natural, but not always the case in the supernatural. When you and I do good deeds or sow seeds, we do so because we were chosen. Not because we were arbitrarily in the right place at the right time.

Deeds are not done arbitrarily. They don't just happen; they have a specific life purpose and you have been chosen to deliver them to their destination. We serve as incubators for our seed until all of the right substance has been gathered. And, at the right moment and time, a condition will occur to enable the deliverance. Everything happens for the benefit of change. The acceleration of change is determined by our awareness of its existence. The more you understand, the more you put into practice. So maybe reaping what we sow could better be described as reaping what we know.

The best part about sowing seeds is that 80 percent of it is without our knowledge. For instance, a smile or a thank you could have been what made the difference today in someone's life.

Don't always expect to see the benefit of a good deed, because sometimes they are like illnesses that go undiagnosed because they are not visible on the surface. This is probably where I should stop because anything on a spiritual level can only be revealed through divine wisdom. Once this concept is fully comprehended, you will immediately be launched into a new path and a new awareness.

In my preparation to close, I want to share something that happened to me in the wee hours of the morning. I was awakened as though someone had called my name. The sowing seed thoughts started filtering through my mind. For writing purposes, I keep paper and pen close by at night. On this particular night I was awakened and led to write:

> **The seeds that I'm going to sow today,**
> **Let them fall on good ground,**
> **And be pleasing in your sight,**
> **And bring forth good fruits.**
> **Bless me to be able to sow many more seeds,**
> **in the days,**
> **weeks and months to come.**

When I finished writing, my thoughts were "I will use this as my daily intention" and I went back to sleep. The next morning, I looked at the writing and the first thing that came to mind was, "All of your needs and desires will be met as long as they include meeting the needs of others."

I'm sure a lot of you have had similar incidents that were clear to you that something was trying to get your attention. To be chosen to sow a seed reveals that God has found favor with you. It is now clearer to me that sowing seeds is not only for the benefit of the receiver, but it's an act of obedience that puts you in covenant with God. The message I wrote that night has since lived out its true meaning. Let me share how it has unfolded in my life. The first part, "The seed that I'm going to sow today" represents change. My intention is met by God's universal plan. Next part "Let them fall on good ground" represents healing and strength. All is well with my soul. Next part, "And to be pleasing in your sight", is acknowledging it's God's plan. My plan can only last for a season. But a plan orchestrated by God will serve a lifetime. Last part, "And bring forth good fruits", harvests time. Process completed, job well done. Your unselfish act to others puts you in God's unlimited favors. We long to be the whole person, having wisdom at its fullness and understanding with its greatness. Make every day your intention to add value to someone else's life. Because in doing so you change your own.

My Testimony

• • • • • •

A testimony is an undeniable experience that's meant for the benefit of others. Healing is not something I pray for; sickness is something I do not accept.

--Herman Hall

Chapter | # My Testimony

W e all are familiar with the scripture: "we are healed by His stripes." Should I understand that to say I will never get sick because the price has already been paid? If I do get sick and go to the doctor, have I made Christ's suffering in vain? The list of questions is too long to mention them all. You're never going to understand the meaning behind that scripture by just using human logic. I say that to say if God was that easy to figure out, then we could have created the earth and all of its habitats. If you want to understand God, you will probably have to get it straight from Him. Only God has a way of revealing Himself to you that goes far beyond any other capability that exists. His revelation comes from a depth that only He can reach - from the seed of the soul. My personal testimony of how I was healed helped me to understand how things are uniquely designed just for us.

About two years prior to this writing, during one of my yearly physical exams, I was diagnosed with high blood pressure. I was stunned to hear that I had high blood pressure, especially with the workout routines I was performing daily. The doctor thought the level was too risky to let it go untreated, so I was put on medication. After two weeks, I went back for a follow-up appointment and, to my surprise, the doctor had to put me on a second medication because the pressure was still too high. I asked the doctor why this was occurring since I was in good physical condition. I never smoked, didn't drink and wasn't overweight. The doctor said that in spite of my athleticism, my condition must be hereditary. They decided, with a little encouragement from me, to do several other tests just to make sure there weren't problems in any other area. Everything checked out. I had no choice but to accept their findings and take the medications. On top of the two medications working on my psyche, it was costing me over $200 every three months.

Regardless of what the doctor said, in my heart I never really accepted that nothing could be done. To me, it just didn't make sense. I said to myself that there has to be a way to change this. But we kept coming back to the same solution; you have it because your parents had it. I just wasn't ready to accept that. I prayed about it, talked with God -- no change. I increased my workout -- no change. I made more changes to my diet -- no change. So that summer, I packed up my computers and took them to my sister's place to work from there for a few weeks.

Before my arrival at my sister's place, my brother-in-law had found and brought home an old elliptical machine. I don't know why they had it because they sure weren't [didn't] using it (smile). The resistant part of the machine (the part where you could increase the resistance) was broken. You could still use it but the level of resistance stayed the same. They told me they were pretty much forced to take the machine from the owner. They really didn't see any need to take it because working out wasn't something they were into. But they brought it home anyway. And having no space in the house, they stored it in the garage.

One day while I was getting ready for the gym, they mentioned they had this machine in the garage. They didn't even know what the name of the machine was. I checked it out and saw it was an elliptical machine. So I started using it in the morning to burn off some calories and for cardiovascular. I used it vigorously for about an hour each morning. One morning after a workout, I became very dizzy. I had to sit down to keep from collapsing. After a couple of mornings of this, I checked my blood pressure with a monitor I had purchased and my pressure was very low. I didn't know what to do or what to think. So I got this thought to stop taking one of the medications and see if that would help. It did help; the pressure was still a little low, but I was no longer getting dizzy after workouts. After returning home from my sister's place, I made an appointment to tell my doctor what had happened.

The doctor said to continue taking the one medication for now and see what happened. In the meantime, I was out looking around at a fitness store and they had this nice, heavy-duty elliptical machine someone had returned to the store. I inquired about it and the sales person said that it was a return product but practically new. He said if I were interested in purchasing it, he would give me 10 percent off. I had gotten used to the one at my sister's place by the time I left there. So I went ahead and bought it. A couple of months later, the blood pressure was still fine. I told the doctor that I believed that I could come off the rest of the medication. The doctor said she would give me a prescription to use only if I needed to. I had the prescription filled, but haven't had to use it as of the day of this writing. So what do you think?

Here are the facts: I had high blood pressure that runs in the family, I was in the best of shape, I didn't have a lot of salt intake, I ate my share of fruits and vegetables, I wasn't overweight, I had an excellent workout routine, numerous tests were done and everything checked out. End result:
My brother-in-law brought an elliptical machine home that they never used. I visited my sister's and started using their broken elliptical machine and blood pressure started dropping. I went from two medications to none, and returned home to find another elliptical machine in a store that had been returned. Those are the facts.

I was never interested in an elliptical machine before I visited my sister. In the gym after a workout, I would get on the treadmill for a cool down.

So was my brother-in-law supposed to bring that machine home? Was I supposed to go visiting at their place at that time to use it? Was the elliptical machine part of the solution? If you're wondering what I believe, I'm about to tell you. Too many things had to happen to be coincidental. The timing and all the other events surrounding that trip were too structured to just be a coincidence. Do I believe that God had anything to do with it? That answer is yes, and why He chose to do it that way, I don't know. Looking back, I can now see that my healing was not just for the high blood pressure.

There are things you don't realize at the time but in retrospect it all becomes clear. Did God need the help of an elliptical machine to heal me? Did He need the children of Israel to march around the walls of Jericho to help Him bring down the wall? Did He need the people to put water in the vessel in order for Him to turn the water into wine? Did He need Moses to put a tree branch in the water to change it from bitter to sweet? Couldn't He have brought the walls of Jericho down without the march? Couldn't He have just spoken the word to the water vessel and made wine without having the pots filled? Couldn't He have made the water sweet without the tree branch? Yes, He could have done all those things without any problem, including bringing high blood pressure down without the help of an elliptical machine. What I realize is that if those things had not happened, God would not have gotten the credit.

Whenever there's a divine intervention, the scripture makes it clear that these things were done to build the faith of those that were involved and to those that were around. Everything that happens to us is uniquely structured just for us. Someone else may be cured from high blood pressure from walking or standing. Maybe that's a way of getting through to them to help them in other areas. When these types of things happen, they are in accordance with what you are in need of. It wasn't just the elliptical machine, but it was the driving there, the place where it happened, the people that were around and for the purpose of this writing. I realize now that the thought to not accept what the doctor said was part of the process. I'm sure I probably thought it was me, but in retrospect, I can see that the whole process was put together for me. The single biggest mistake I was about to make was to think that this battle was mine to fight. It took all that to happen just for me to understand who really was in charge. That was what I needed to happen in order for me to be able to understand the lesson that was being taught. Everyone's lesson is different. The lesson with the wall of Jericho, with the wine vessel, and turning the water from bitter to sweet was for those that were there.

In the beginning of this section, I said God would supply all my needs according to His will. The operative words are, His will. Too often, we want God's will to be our will. When that doesn't happen, we see little reason to have any faith in God. But how many times have we looked back at something we had asked for and realized that we weren't really ready for it?

And was glad that it didn't happen at the time. Because if it had, everything would have gone wrong.

I want to leave you with this. My healing was not because of my faith, the same as Lazarus was not raised by the faith of the people that were around. If you remember the story, when Jesus arrived, Martha said, "you are too late, Lazarus is dead" (John 11:21). My healing was not because of my faith, but it was to make my faith stronger for the times to come.

The Abraham Effect

• • • • • •

Enthusiasm without passion is a set up for failure. God's favor will bring us through insurmountable obstacle to inconceivable growth.

--Herman Hall

Chapter | **THE ABRAHAM EFFECT**

What is the Abraham Effect? Of all the stories I've read, the life and lifestyle of Abraham and Sarah is probably the one that I most frequently refer to. Primarily it is the unshakable faith Abraham had in God that inspires me. To me, his faith in God made him undoubtedly second to none. He became the father of faith setting the example others go by. He was someone whose faith in God did not waver. Whenever I'm challenged, one of my standard courses of action is to remember Abraham. He became the role model who has added strength to my armor of faith.

Abraham's circumstances never turned him from his faith in God. Too often we lose sight of our vision and abandon our plans during challenging times. What I like about Abraham was that he never lost faith in God's plan. He knew that his fate was not in his hands.

So keeping his faith in God's plan was his only hope of successfully completing his mission. When things got a little confusing, he held on and drew from his inner strength. He never wavered from the orders he was given.

As difficult as challenges can get, we must continue to move toward our vision. Making yourself believe in that which is not, as though it is, is easier said than done. This may be especially difficult when times are not so favorable. Be careful to not empower your circumstances, giving strength to adversity. Focusing or dwelling on an unfavorable situation too long in thought can cause it to appear bigger than what it is. You either eliminate it or figuratively distance yourself from it.

The Abraham effect speaks to me in subliminal messages, telling me that I may not always understand the path that I'm on, but to have faith that the destination is true. This journey has been designed to strengthen our faith. For every stronghold you encounter will always come with its own built in solution. If you miss the solution, you will not permanently remove the stronghold. If you manage to get around the stronghold, you will revisit it and its solution when it reappears further along the path. A student is never given an exam without being given all the possible information to successfully pass it. The universe operates with those same types of laws and principles. Abraham knew that his journey was not all about him. He knew it was more about fulfilling God's plan. And he knew that at any given time (even though/when he didn't understand it), his situation was never out of God's control and never without His divine guidance.

Let me suggest that Abraham had a made up mind from the beginning that regardless of circumstances, he was going to press his way through. When we allow crisis to distort our judgment, fear will find its way in and piece-by-piece take us apart. Once fear is in, it won't stop until it creates gaps in our forward progress. Gaps will cause irregularity, which disrupts the order in the way we do things. If an immediate correction isn't made, then with certainty things will turn chaotic.

Faith can be compared to that same scenario. When we feel that our faith has failed, we become like a person who has just lost their equilibrium. You become unstable. Your thoughts begin to wander, causing your faith to become disoriented. Abraham's situation (at times) wasn't always good. He was faced with challenges like many of us. The one thing Abraham knew was that destiny had come calling and that he couldn't ignore it. The mission wasn't as clear and didn't offer as many comforts as he would have liked, but he had to answer the call. Many of us, at some point, have tried to renege or denounce whether a particular call was for us. But the more we tried to ignore it the more intense the feeling grew. In most cases, we had to finally surrender and begin listening to our inner voice. I have often wondered what assurance Abraham received to confirm leaving home was of God. Is there a way in which we can be absolutely sure God had ordered a change? Many have said it's all in your feeling or your higher consciousness -- that inner voice. Go to my website and send me your thoughts. I would like to hear them. I will say that all of the moves I've made that I feel were part of my path were beyond my comprehension.

So my acting on them came down to my faith. Writing this book is one of them. In either case, doing something out of faith should be done with careful thought. One of the worst things that can happen to a person is to have a responsibility that you're not passionate about. You end up not having the required staying power to endure to the end. And if you are not around to see the end, how will you know if there are any changes you can make to improve your chances? If you know anything about racecar driving, you know that you don't quit the race because you're behind. You stay the course and finish the race. At any given time, anything can happen on the track that could change the outcome of the race. So you have to be patient and keep performing until the race is over.

Too many times we quit short of our victory. Enthusiasm without passion is a set up for failure. Your inner strength, wisdom, understanding and perseverance are products of your passion. Enthusiasm alone is not enough to sustain you. Each time you find a way to make a plan work, your mind seems to come up with other ways to counter it. But what I have learned is that challenges are not always a bad thing nor should they be viewed as a 'set-back'. Many times, it is the unsuccessful challenge today that gives way to the victory tomorrow.

Defeat in some instances can be labeled as an early preempted strike of tomorrow's problem. Defeat in one situation may serve as the motivating factor that got you through other things. In other words, tough love is not always bad.

Sometimes in the midst of your circumstances is where you find your most favorable solution. Abraham knew it was not in his best interest to dwell on circumstances. Uncertainty prohibits movement. There were two very important things Abraham knew. The first was that he knew he had some place to go. He didn't know where, but he knew it was some place. The second was that he knew getting there was not predicated on his ability. Knowing these two things relieved him from the pressure of trying to be in control. He knew that the success of his journey was based on staying with the voice that was guiding him.

How much strain and stress are we subjecting ourselves to? Keep in mind that the only time you're in control is when you give up trying to have control. Control, in many cases, is a figment of our imagination. We don't control, we assist or we manage. The only control you will ever have is the control you have over yourself. Abraham knew his circumstances were out of his hands and beyond his control. Circumstances, in most cases, are due to mismanaged priorities. For instance, there are circumstances and consequences that are due to external factors; the current state of our bad economy is a good example. Though we are affected by the circumstances, we are not guilty of the cause. So in the midst of circumstances, if you want control, then focus on changing the order of the way you do things. Revisit your priorities and make new choices that effect new decisions. So that when the crisis is over, your order of operation is already in place to move forward.

Abraham's main priority was to carry out the order he was given. If you know the story of Abraham, you know he was not exempt from the perils of life. He had to endure normal life circumstances just as you and I. Many of us feel that because we are believers in Christ that our accountability should be different from those of non-believers. Consequences pertaining to earthly laws and principles apply to everyone and everything. You can only be responsible for the action you commit. Your responsibility as a believer is to proactively stop reprimandable actions before they happen. You're not set apart by claiming to be a believer, but you are set apart because of your day-to-day walk. It was Abraham's action that made him different, not just his belief. And it was the challenges he endured that proved his faith. How can you and I know what we are capable of without a challenge to prove it? There has to be some form of testing to determine quality. The level of quality is determined by the degree of testing. If you want to know your potential, then start by looking at the challenges you were able to successfully overcome. Abraham didn't expect or receive any preferential treatment. He was an ordinary man doing practical things on a spiritual journey. All that he couldn't make happen for himself, in the natural, God made happen for him in the super natural. As a carnal man, he lived by the sweat of his brow. But his spiritual man lived and walked in the presence of God. The Abraham Effect has caused me to live more in the here and now. The more I celebrate in the current moment, the more empowered, confident and triumphant I feel. With these variables in place, being victorious in any endeavor is all but inevitable.

Taking time to enjoy what you have makes for a smoother finish for what you're trying to achieve.

As well prepared as Abraham was, it was not long into his journey before something went wrong. Regardless of who we are or what level of faith we have, it will be tested. Abraham's faith was about to be tested when famine struck the land. In order for Abraham to survive the famine, he had to go into Egypt, which caused different concerns and new challenges. In those days, if a man's wife was fair to look on, the husband's life could be in danger, thus causing Abraham to have reason to be afraid because the scripture stated that '....Sarah was pleasant to look on'. The possibility existed that the King of Egypt might greatly desire her. If this were so, Abraham could be killed in order for the king to have her. So now on top of the famine he has to fear for his life. Can you imagine some of the thoughts that must have gone through Abraham's mind? The human side of him had to have been saying, "where did I go wrong? How could this be happening?" Immediately at the first sign of trouble or the first sight of an obstacle, we begin to blame ourselves for the situation. "Had I not been incompetent or inadequate, this would not be happening" is what we say to ourselves. We should view challenges as an opportunity for growth -- not a sign of defeat. By now, Abraham's mind is starting to play games with him. I'm sure he's thinking to himself, "....God I hope that this journey I'm on includes protecting me."

Have you ever found yourself in a situation and reality begins to set in? And everything seems to be pointing toward an unavoidable disaster? Time, effort and money seem all but gone.

My guess is these are the type of thoughts Abraham was dealing with. To Abraham, it felt like Egypt had just handed him a damp blanket on a cold night. But the Abraham Effect was still in place. Do you know what happens when you spend too much time thinking about a plan that's not working? You don't give the one that will work a chance to get in. After you have given a nonproductive idea a reasonable amount time, you have to free up resources for something else. Otherwise, days later you will find yourself still going back and forth without any significant progress. What Abraham, you and I sometimes seem to forget is that what seems to be an ending for us is only the beginning for God. Sometimes we have to lose our way so God can become our way. And I mean that literally. Most of us can recall moments when we had to rely on the Abraham Effect. We all have had times when life gave us more questions than answers; more problems than solutions. In some of my quiet time, I used to wonder why we have to have challenges. Was there any good reason for having them? And somewhere in the stillness of time an answer breached my thoughts, revealing to me that every time I had a challenge; God knew that I would get a chance to know Him better each time He delivered me. Things don't always happen for the reason we think they do. If you think about it, what would be the use of a challenge if you didn't learn anything from it? We need to have the mindset that anything that challenges us is here to teach us. And everything that's here to teach us is here to advance us.

Abraham's plan was to stay in Egypt until the famine was over. God's plan was to challenge him first and then advance him.

He was challenged (to save his life) by saying that Sarah was his sister and not his wife. God's plans was to have Sarah untouched by the Egyptian and have Abraham leave Egypt richer than when he came in. When Abraham's plan seemed to have come to its end, God's plan was just beginning. After 99 years, Abraham and Sarah were finally blessed with their first son. And after their son was of age, it was time for Abraham to be promoted again. He was told to offer up his son as a sacrifice. Though he was filled with pain, and had no reasonable understanding for God's request, he prepared his son for the sacrifice. But once again God had His own plan. Not only did God provide the sacrificial lamb and spare Abraham's son, He also made a covenant with him. In His covenant God said, "...because of your faith, you will be the father of many nations, and their numbers will be as the sands of the sea". Today we are the seeds of Abraham, heirs to the promises that were made because of the Abraham Effect.

What is the Abraham Effect? It is the sustainment of life through knowing the divine providence and power of God.

Breaking Free From Trenches
To New Birth

. . . . . .

*Transformation doesn't just
happen. It doesn't just show up
and force itself on us. Condition
and position play a major role.
One of the required conditions is
to understand where you are and
where you're going.*

--Herman Hall

Chapter 10 | CONCLUSION

We have covered many thought provoking ideas that will serve as reminders during uncertain times. In closing, I want to say that the children of Israel were camped out in the wilderness right next door to the promise land for 40 years. Where are we camped out? Are our dreams, goals or accomplishments right around the corner? We know why the wilderness was home for the Israelites for so long. They didn't have faith to receive what was already given to them. What gifts and talents are already promised to us? How much faith and trust do we put in them? Are we spending too much time camped out in circumstances, unworthiness, unbelief or challenges? What condition has become a stronghold that we need to be set free from? Whereever you're camped out or whatever Trench you need freedom from, just stand up, and many times you will discover that it's only knee deep.

Sometimes having blinders on will cause us to keep our eyes closed even when the blinders come off. Blinders can cause us to think that we really can't see or we use blinders as an excuse to have nothing expected from us by others. Break camp! It's time for new possibilities. Overcome where you are and choose where you want to go. How do you do this? You do this by being grateful for the process that it took to set you free. Many times we interchange the word freedom with deliverance. You can be delivered from something without having the full appreciation of being there. But the process of freedom leaves reminders of what the situation was like and what it took to be free of it. While you were there, the situation served its purpose of making sure you stayed away.

Transformation doesn't just happen. It doesn't just show up and force itself on us. Condition and position play a major role. One of the required conditions is to understand where you are and where you're going. You need to know that your purpose in life is not about exhausting yourself to find what life has to offer. It's about surrendering yourself to hear what life has to say. If you have been in a trench, you are now prepared to come out.

Sometime it's the order in which things are done. For too long, we have had good intention, but are working in the wrong order. I don't hear much said about order. But as there is wisdom, there is an order in which we receive wisdom. You don't just wake up one morning with great wisdom.

Things have to be done and lessons have to be learned for wisdom to be received. God had an order during creation. He didn't create the fish before the water. He didn't create man before first creating a place for him to stay and food for him to eat. Order has its place and purpose in all things. What order is applied when it comes to prosperity? How many times have we known of prosperous people that end up not so prosperous? Order has a major role in prosperity. Many of us desired wealth without first gaining wisdom. We went after wealth without going after understanding. Some of us go as far as going after wealth at the expense of our own health. Without proper health, wisdom and understanding, you will never properly manage your wealth. Prosperity is about increase. And true prosperity or increase should be visible in every area of our lives. Without all the components of prosperity, health, wisdom and understanding, we operate in deficit mode because of the lack of knowledge. Again, that may not be through any fault of yours. You may not have known the importance of order. Before you go after wealth, go after health, wisdom and understanding first. They are the mechanisms that keep the order that continue the increase.

Change is not always the easiest thing to do. If we could somehow find a way to reap the benefit, without investing any time in change, that would be a more favorable option. Perhaps if we could get a different perspective of change, it would help. Instead of viewing change as something we make happen, let's look at change as something we let happen.

It's already done. We talked about the power of words. The one thought I want to emphasize is that we are connected to what we say more than we know. Words have the power to create conditions that become our circumstances. Life and death is in the power of words. Change your words and you change your experiences.

Let's not forget the seed. Make it your intention to sow seeds every day. Sowing seed is an act of love, in any form, and a measure of faith. Your seed should always be to add value to others. When you sow a seed, it puts you in alignment with God's covenant. Your seed is transformed from an act of obedience to an abundance of God's favor. A seed sown with the right motive brings the right manifestation.

How can I close without mentioning vision? Vision is like an engine. It will take you as far as you can see -- as far as you want to go. But when your vision becomes distorted, negative perception, low self-esteem and your self-confidence become victims. A distorted vision will take you off course and take you out of your purpose.

And last, but not least, is the Abraham Effect. For if God is my source, then I'm never without resource.

A NOTE FROM THE AUTHOR

Become a student to your passion in life. You don't have to be an expert; you just have to be committed and dedicated. Make ample time to discover how vast and deep your potentials are. Don't be afraid to entertain what you can't explain. None of us knows what's inside of us waiting to give birth. Don't delay your gift for fear of being judged by those that don't understand the process. That's an old trick of the enemy to make you feel inadequate so that your dreams will never become a reality. Significance and purpose is all about mindset. Changing your way of thinking creates a new life of purpose. You have to get beyond having a reasonable explanation for everything that happens. We don't live to understand the next thing that's going to happen; we live to be the next thing that's going to happen. Too often, we take on the role of the scavenger when we should have the mindset of a creator. A scavenger collects things that have been discarded, whereas a creator is discarding things to make room for new discoveries. Make this your day of change and work with whatever gift you have even though to you it may seen small. Small things done with great love will produce great results.

About the Author

Herman Hall is a visionary. He accredits his gift of vision to his early childhood experience where he dedicated most of his time as a musician in his local church. His gift in music would lead him to his own gospel quartette and their own Sunday morning radio show. At an early age, he was instrumental in assisting his pastor in the teaching ministries. He went on to travel the country during his military career and gained a much broader knowledge of other ethnic groups. After his military career, he asserted himself as a computer engineer where he was one of the technical gurus of his time. His quests for accomplishment went on to include becoming an independent trader on Wall Street. But then he discovered in a unique way that God had given him wisdom to use for inspirational purposes. Many motivational speakers and teachers became his mentors and were a huge benefactor to his finding his purpose in writing.

Contact the Author at:

www.hermanhall.com
www.investedmind.net
email: hermanhall8@aol.com